Make Money Online. From Zero To Domination. A Step By Step Guide On How To Build A Killer Online Business and Create Massive Amounts Of Wealth Starting Today!

Kevin Hughes Copyright © 2015

Table of Contents

The Basics

Conclusion

Congratulations!

Thanks for purchasing my book. This guide is a detailed process on how to start your internet business from scratch and build it into a full blown online empire. I'll show you how even the newest Internet rookies can begin earning money online and turn that money into a successful and wildly profitable online business.

The Basics

This is not a get rich quick system! Like anything worthwhile in life this will require time and work on your part. Don't worry if you don't have a lot of time to devote to this. You can work this at whatever pace you feel comfortable with. Some will have only a few hours a week to spend while others may have 80 hrs a week to spend on it. Everyone is different.

1. Whether you grow at a slow or fast pace the important thing is you continue to grow your business. Don't be weighed down by indecision! This can be a paralyzing trap many newbie's fall into. Make a plan of action and stick to it. One of my favorite time management and goal setting techniques is the Pomodoro Method which you can find tutorials of online.

2. Always be learning! The more you allow yourself to be open to new ideas and the more you dive into the process, the quicker you'll get to where you want to be and the more successful you'll become. The Internet is constantly evolving so you need to evolve with it or risk being left behind. Stay up to date on what methods and techniques your peers and mentors are employing to continue being successful. Take advantage of Facebook Groups and forums.

3. Everything you earn in the early stages you need to reinvest into your growing business. I can't stress the importance of this step! I know your first urge might be to cash out and use this money for other things. **I GET THAT!** But you need to look at this from the viewpoint of a long term investment. The more you put into it the more you'll get out of it. This guide is truly showing you how to start at $0 and work your way up the ladder to living a life of financial freedom. If you don't have any other income and need to take money out in order to survive expect your progress to be much slower. I use GoDaddy Bookkeeping to track all my income and expenses.

4. Take massive action! Too many people buy courses and books like this and never lift a finger to implement them. People with a "Can Do" attitude go much farther in life and in business than people who always say "I Can't". Your mind is your most powerful weapon! Most people get frustrated and quit at the first roadblock. Bust through these mental barriers and you'll be much better off for it.

If you have some money to spend, then you may want to skip a few of the initial money earners I'll lay out in Stage #1 and #2. That's fine, but you still need to continue to reinvest your profits back into growing your business.

Once you're making a healthy amount every month you can decide to continue to reinvest it all or begin systematically keeping a larger portion for yourself each month. Money management is a key part of being successful. The more responsibly you manage your money the quicker you'll get to where you want to be financially. Most people neglect this aspect and it ends up costing them.

It's not just about making money it's all about making the money you already made work for you!

When I started I used the JARS Method Of Money Management. The basic premise is to create a number of jars that you would set aside a certain percentage of money into each month totaling a 100%. Since I was keeping this online business start up completely separate from my other finances I had to readjust what each of the JARS was for.

As time passes you may want to add employees or you may want to start saving some of the money instead of reinvesting. Simply adjust, add or subtract your JARS accordingly.

This example is what I started off with. Mine has changed over time. Feel free to set up your system however you think works best for your business. I urge you to use some form of money management. The more processes you have set firmly in place, the smoother, more efficient, and profitable your business will run. Having processes in place not only leads to more production but also less money wasted.

JARS System

Tools & Trackers – 10% – This fund is for any tools or services I wanted to purchase to help grow and manage my businesses. For example: getting a paid version of GoDaddy Bookkeeping or Long Tail Pro.

Education - 10% - Learning is crucial in the online game. What worked a few years ago may no longer work or even exist today. Use this fund for books, courses & mastermind groups to help you further your business

New Business Development - 20% – Any start up costs in each new venture you add to your portfolio. Use these funds for those beginning costs to get up and running. For example: buying domain names and outsourcing any work you're unable or unwilling to do when building a niche site.

Continuing Business Development - 40% – These are the ongoing costs for your established businesses. For example: Buying inventory for your established eBay or Amazon business.

Marketing & Promotion - 15% – These are costs for getting your businesses out in front of the buying public. For example: Paying a virtual assistant to promote your site or product.

Miscellaneous – 5% – Anything not falling into these categories. For example: This could be savings for a new computer or printer. Basically anything involving your business that isn't covered above.

Stage #1 - Beginning at Zero!

Tired of working your same dead end job? Want to quit and work for yourself but don't know how?

Well if you've ever felt this way then you're just like I was a few years ago. I used to work as a Manager at a big emergency call center. Needless to say, this job came with a lot of stress and a lot of time away from my friends and family. I dreamed of creating my own job and working for myself. I longed for the freedom of making my own schedule and calling the shots in my life. It took me a long time, filled with a lot of trial and error to figure out a method that worked for me.

Now, over the last four years I've become my own boss and I've made a good living using the techniques and tricks I'm going to share with you here. My journey is by no way complete! I've had some setbacks, but I learned to adapt and persevere. While I've attained my original goals of working for myself and becoming financially independent I continue to create new and exciting goals to propel me to even greater heights! Soon enough you will too!

So enough about me! Here are a few easy and free ways to make some initial start up cash online. Like I mentioned above if you already have some cash feel free to skip this step but I know many of you might be struggling and these are excellent ways to inject some steady cash into your new business.

*If you don't already have one you'll need to open up a PayPal account and add in your banking information. If you plan on running a business online PayPal is going to be a vital part of your business. Be sure to read their policy and guidelines carefully. I've heard of people violating their terms of services and having their accounts locked. Things like that can cripple your new business if you're not careful. There are a variety of other online payment processors but Paypal is the big dog and the one I have personal experience with. If you can make it work with another processor than by all means do what's right for you.

The Stage #1 Goal:

The goal of this section is to earn at least $800 to $1000 dollars. This will be your initial cash reserves and will allow you to later reinvest in some of things you'll need in future stages. Now while there's nothing stopping you from moving on to other sections before you've made this much you should continue using these areas, or at the very least use them as source of revenue anytime you're start to run low on funds.

Personally I never liked to get below $500 dollars when I was at this stage. Remember these are free or low cost areas of quick revenue that will always be available to you. Use them to really get a jump start on your online business.

I would also like to mention that this is not a race! The best way to build a solid foundation is to do things one thing at a time. Don't try to jump ahead too quickly and do everything at once. Many people fail because of their lack of patience and self control. The more disciplined you are the better off you'll be.

eBay

Make some quick cash by starting your own eBay business. Just create an account, familiarize yourself with the site and begin selling. You can begin with items from around your house that you no longer want or you can go to sites like Craigslist and look under the FREE section for items you think you can make a profit on.

To begin with, eBay will only let you list a few items every month and they will hold your money until items are delivered. However, after about 60 days in good standing, you'll begin to receive payment immediately and you can request your selling limits be increased.

Once you've sold a few things take the money you've earned and reinvest it back into some more items to sell. Do this until you've built up some inventory. Then, begin to reinvest a portion back into growing your eBay business while also saving a percentage for some of the things we'll discuss later on this guide.

Many people run successful eBay businesses, either part time or full time. It's a great way to start building wealth for bigger future projects. You can find a wealth of knowledge online.. Personally, I subscribe to a lot of YouTube channels that specialize in reselling and watch videos while working on other online projects.

Be careful when setting your shipping prices. There's nothing worse than losing money on shipping because you weren't paying attention to how much an item you're selling weighs. If in doubt use the USPS Postage Calculator to help you figure it out.

I prefer using eBay labels and printing out my shipping online. You get a pretty substantial discount on most forms of shipping when you do this. Also, if you're sending out a priority package many areas will actually offer FREE Home pickup, saving you a trip to the Post Office. Just type "USPS Schedule Pickup" into Google and that should bring up the link to the form. Click on it and start filling out the Schedule Pickup form to see if you're in an available area. The post office also offers a wide array of FREE supplies. Check them out at the USPS website

Places to Find Items:

Garage Sales - (Find on Craigslist / Your local classifieds / Garage Sales phone apps)

Flea Markets - (Most areas have at least one / Look up online)

Estate Sales - (Find on Craigslist / Your local classifieds / Estatesales.net)

Thrift Stores - (Goodwill / Salvation Army)

Auctions - (Find online and offline auctions listed on sites like Auctionzip)

Retail Stores - (Retail Arbitrage / Clearance Items)

Online - (Sites like eBay ShopGoodwill.com, Craigslist)

Amazon (Merchant Fulfilled or FBA)

Amazon is another great platform to sell new and secondhand goods. It's the same basic premise as eBay with a different interface & fee structure, a focus on newer items and the addition of FBA program. Amazon is a popular place for retail arbitrage and really heats up during the 4th quarter especially when it comes to Toys and Kids items. You'll find some items sell quicker and for more money on each of the different platforms so having both an Amazon and eBay account is a smart idea.

Amazon has two main options which is to either manually fulfill orders yourself or take advantage of Fulfilled by Amazon (FBA) and have them send out your items, deal with customer emails and returns. Each one has its pros and cons so do your research and see which one fits your lifestyle best.

** Amazon FBA has a higher learning curve at first but there's tons of resources out there to walk you through your first shipment including a series of videos by Amazon itself.

** Eventually once you've got some money to reinvest you can even begin to experiment with creating your own Private Label product listings.

Craigslist

Craigslist is an excellent place not only to buy items to flip for a profit but also sell items. Craigslist is a local directory where people can search for local items in a variety of categories. You then contact one another, agree on a price and meet up to finish the deal. Personally, I use this more for buying then selling but I do use Craigslist to move heavier and bulkier items that don't make sense to ship using a site like eBay or Amazon.

Some other alternatives:

Etsy
Bonanza
Gumtree

Content Writing Cash Flow

What is content writing? Well it's basically writing articles or blog posts for other people in exchange for money. This is a great way to get started earning some extra cash. You can easily earn a few hundred dollars a month or more depending on your level of writing ability and time you want to invest. Content writing will help you generate money to begin funding your new online business. You can go into Google and find quite a few of these sites.

My personal favorite is Text Broker Unlike some of the other content writing sites out there Text Broker has a quick and easy application process which means you'll be earning money in no time. You can request a payment be made to your PayPal account once a week as long as you have more than $10 in your account. I've made thousands of dollars using this site and you can too. By all means feel free to apply to as many of these content writing sites as possible. This will only increase the amount of money you can potentially make. Be warned that many have more involved application processes and stricter standards for accepting new writers. That's why I suggest starting with Text Broker, Upwork and Elance.

Some other options:

Many of these sites are geared towards specific niches so you'll need to sort through them and find which ones fit your personal style of writing and interests. As with all of these services content must be a 100% original.

Listverse
iWriter
Hubpages
Elance
Upwork
Writers Weekly
ACHS
Top Tenz
Funds For Writers
Doctor Of Credit
Lab Mice
Be A Freelance Blogger
The Dollar Stretcher

Writers.ph
The Penny Hoarder
Freelancer Careers
eCommerce Insiders
BootsnAll
Transitions Abroad
YourOnline.biz
A Fine Parent
Matador
Treehouse
The Travel Writers Life
Ux Booth
Write Naked
Cracked
Digital Ocean
Metro Parent
Tuts+ Code
Tuts+ WP
Tuts+ Vector
Smashing Magazine
A List Apart
Ontext
Sitepoint
International Living
Funny Times

*** A good resource for checking your content to make sure it's not plagiarized or copied is Copyscape Premium. It only costs .05 cents per check and you should run all of you're articles through it before submitting finished work to any of the above sites. Better to be safe then sorry!

**Upwork and Elance are also great if you have technical skills or experience using certain type of software and digital programs. You can also find jobs on there for graphic design, editing, and working as a virtual assistant. These sites provide a lot of flexibility and are potential goldmines if you have some online skills.

The Power of Fiverr and Gigbucks

Fiverr and Gigbucks are two popular sites where you can offer any service you can think up for $5 or more. These sites are excellent for people just starting out with no money to invest. Just visit these sites and browse around to get an idea of the different services people are offering. Of course if you have a special talent like SEO skills or writing skills you can advertise those, but you can also get more creative and offer to sing happy birthday to anyone or listen to a person's problem and give them sound advice. The ideas are really limitless!

Here a few quick suggestions for gigs!

1. Product Reviewer - This is a simple gig to get started with. Tons of people need reviews for their products and services. After all reviews are often the main factor that convinces buyers into purchasing a product from you rather than from the other guy. If the product is something like an eBook just ask for a free copy so you can review it. Make sure you direct them to your blog or Facebook page. Somewhere they can send you the file for the product that needs reviewing. Remember these sites don't allow people to share email addresses with one another on their sites. After you've looked over the product then write your review. If you want to get a leg up on the competition you can also tell the buyer you'll post the review on all of your social media pages like Twitter, Facebook, and YouTube (video reviews).

2. Social Promoter – Create a bunch of different social media accounts (Digg, Twitter, Facebook, Instagram, StumbleUpon, Blogger, and YouTube). Next start to gain some followers on each. You can help this process by doing things like Digging your other social media pages, Tweeting about your other social media pages, and Liking them on Facebook. Once you've got some followers create a gig offering to promote someone's message on all your social media accounts. By offering to promote them on multiple sites they are getting more bang for their buck by choosing your gig.

3. Unique, Funny, Weird and Crazy – I touched on this above but the more inventive and wild you are with the gigs you offer the more you stand out from other sellers. Just use your imagination. You can basically sell anything on these sites. If you can dream it then offer it as a gig. You never know what gig is going to take off.

When offering gigs you may also want to offer a free gift for purchasing. You can tailor it to the gig you're offering or it can be something silly that you attach to all your gigs. People love free stuff and by offering them a free gift you're adding perceived value to your gig. One example is offering a free report or guide. This can either be something you've created yourself or a PLR (Private Label Rights) report you've purchased and can sell.

These sites let you offer around 20 active gigs at one time and I would highly suggest coming up with 20 different things you can offer. That way you've got as many chances to earn as possible. Not only that but when people click on one of your gigs they can see other gigs you offer. Even though they might not be interested in the original gig they may want to purchase something else.

Also remember to sell yourself when writing these gigs. Show them everything you have to offer and how it will benefit them to buy from you.

Make sure to create gigs that won't take you hours to complete. The quicker your gig can be accomplished the more you earn for your time. If it takes over 20 minutes it might be a good idea to think of something else. The exception to this is for gigs that you're offering for prices higher than $5.

Be sure to up sell. Each gig is $5 dollars but you can break down more time consuming and complicated work into multiple gigs. You can also make separate gigs for things like rush delivery. Be sure to take advantage of this when creating your gigs. The more options you give potential customers the more opportunity you give yourself to make money.
Always leave a link to your site in the gig description! This builds trust and credibility which will help you convert casual lookers into buyers. If you don't have a site, then you can either create a new one around your gigs or start a free blog. I personally prefer to use an actual website. I want things to look as professional as possible for people thinking about purchasing one of my gigs.

Don't forget the importance of tags when creating your gigs. Tags are the terms that people use to find things on these sites. A good tip is to find similar gigs from top sellers and see the types of tags their using. If you're product is unique then think of the terms you would use to try and find it on the site.

When creating your gig I would also suggest using video if possible. Many people are visual and gigs using video convert at a higher rate than gigs without video. Just be yourself and tell people about your gig, the benefits, and why they should purchase from you. There's no need to get fancy when simple will do just fine!

Once you've offered up all the gigs you can it's time to **PROMOTE PROMOTE PROMOTE!!** I don't care what you use whether it's Instagram, Twitter, Facebook, YouTube, or an online forum! Just make sure your gigs get out to people who might be interested in your service. After many sales and many satisfied customers your gigs and you as a seller will build a reputation and you will eventually no longer need to advertise as much!

These sites, especially Fiverr, are a great way to earn some cash. I highly recommend them! You're missing out on an opportunity if you don't.

If you want to go crazy and boost your profits even more, then here's a list of a few other sites that allow you to offer gigs. Setting up your gigs on each of these sites might take a day or so but you'll also be in front of a much wider audience.

1. **SEO Clerks**
2. **Tenrr**
3. **Fourerr**
4. **Fiverup**

Microworkers and Amazon Mechanical Turk

Microworkers and Amazon Mechanical Turk offer you the ability to make money by doing short, quick tasks for money. Some of these tasks include making comments on blogs or YouTube videos, liking Facebook Pages, becoming a follower on someone's twitter account, posting reviews, taking surveys and signing up to websites. While you won't make a ton of cash on these sites what you do make will start to add up pretty quickly if you stick with it.

In the future you might want to use these sites to outsource some of your more basic tasks. Just keep these sites in the back of your mind as they are a great source of inexpensive labor!

Kickstarter

Have a great idea but no capital to get it off the ground. If so, try launching a Kickstarter campaign. This site has grown into the largest funding online platform for creative ideas and projects. From music and movies to games and toys, if you have a good idea and the motivation to see it brought to market, then, this might be an option to explore.

When building your project page you'll want to keep a few things in mind.

Start Planning Months In Advance – Most projects are funded before they even start. What I mean by this is successful project managers do the heavy lifting well in advance. Once it's time for the project to start the word should already be out about your project.

Research Other Successful Projects - Find what worked for others and try to implement or improve upon it for your campaign.

Set a Goal For The Lowest Amount You Can Manage – Don't overshoot. Kickstarter is an all in platform. You either reach your goal and get funded or you don't and get nothing. One alternative to Kickstarter where you can get projects only partially funded and still receive funds is Indiegogo.

Make Your Project Look Professional – You'll want to create a professional looking video. Be sure to proofread any copy you write for spelling and grammar errors. Don't overlook the design of your logos and images. People on Kickstarter care about these things when putting down their money.

Be Creative As Possible - The more unique and memorable you make your project look to potential backers the more likely you're going to capture an audience and get your project funded.

Have Your Ducks In A Row – Be sure to have all the details of your project hammered out in advance. There's nothing worse than asking for money and not being able to answer simple questions regarding your business model. Be sure know to have your expenses for the project figured out including the cost of your perks.

Offer Cool Perks & Stretch Goals – Give people a reason to pay more. If you want people to shell out their hard earned money you better be offering them something amazing in return. I also suggest offering a lot of interesting smaller rewards to draw more people to your project. Also once you reach your goals try offering discounts and bundles in order to reward backers and bring in new backers.

Include Your Budget – People like to see where the money is going. The more you can show them the better.

Keep Your Campaign at Under 30 Days – Statistically projects that are longer than this have a lower success rate.

Reach out to People Before Launching – Reaching 20% funded is considered a tipping point when it comes to getting a project funded. People who reach this number are close to 80% successful in seeing their entire project funded. That means get whoever you can on board.. Whether it's friends, family, business contacts or your email list be sure to reach out in advance and get them excited to support your project.

Stage #2 - You've Made A Few Bucks Now Make A Few More!

This is still the beginning stages. They only difference here is that you may need to or choose to outsource work or purchase some services while doing these tasks that will help you in saving time and becoming more profitable.

Stage #2 Goal

This stage will help you start monetizing some of the big social media outlets. In this stage there are a few tools and services I suggest buying as they will help you make more money and save you a ton of work. Continue working some of your Stage #1 revenue streams and just add these to the mix. Once you've made another $1000 after expenses you should have enough to really dive in to Stage #3 full blast.

You can get started with Stage #3 earlier while you work on Stage #2. For example if you want to do everything yourself you won't need as much capital. I suggest following through on these steps either way as there's a great deal of potential money to be made in the social media universe.

Amazon Kindle Publishing

Kindle Publishing is an excellent way to make some extra income with low initial investment. Depending on your skill set you can actually write and create you e-book for free.. Personally, I write a lot of my e-books but have the cover and proofreading sourced out to others. You can choose to do as much or as little as you'd like depending on what you're willing to spend. Go to a site like Upwork to find a good e-book writer and a site like Fiverr to get your book proofread, formatted or front cover created.

After you're book is finished and uploaded onto Kindle be sure to upload your book to Createspace for people who want a physical copy and ACX for those who like to listen to their content. The sites are both pretty straight forward and will help walk you through the process. There's also a ton of great communities and podcasts dedicated to all three of these publishing avenues, so if you ever get stuck someone will be able to help.

This is a great source of additional income as once the initial work is done there's not much you need to do other than occasionally run promotions and promote your books. I also like to change things up every few months, especially if sales have fallen off on a particular book. When that happens I like to create a new cover and sometimes even a new title for the book. I also will experiment with changing up the keywords I'm targeting and the categories I have the book listed in.

There a lot of great Amazon Kindle Facebook groups. Some offer chances for promotion and FREE review swaps and others are geared towards answering questions and helping people who run into problems. I highly recommend joining a few and learning as much as possible. Even if you're books are only making a little bit each month, once you've got a lot of books published those numbers will quickly begin to add up to serious amounts.

In general, you'll find some books take off and make a killing each month with minimal work, some will bring an average amount with some occasional tweaking and some will struggle to make sales no matter how much work you put into them.

Some tips for Kindle Book Publishers:

1. Make a Plan and Take Action – Figure out what your plan is and take massive action.

Do you want to do everything yourself?
Should I outsource some or all of the books?
How do you plan on marketing the books once finished?
Are you going to use a pen name?
What types of books should I write?

Those are just a few of the many questions you'll want to ask yourself. Personally, since I write all my own e-books I like to break it down into smaller goals. Each day I try and finish 3-4 chapters of a book. This allows me to write a couple books a week without feeling overwhelmed. Maybe your goal will be to do less or to do more. The important thing is taking action everyday and working on your highest leverage activities (or the activities that have the most impact on your business).

2. Quality of Quantity – Amazon want fresh engaging content. The more you provide this the better your book will be in the long run. Amazon is constantly evaluating there system and making changes to ensure quality content. Poor quality content hurts makes Amazon look bad so while you may still make a profit with lower quality books, odds are as they tighten the reigns those books will get pushed down in the rankings no longer making you money.

3. Keyword Research – Use Amazon Bestsellers, Google Trends and a keyword tool to help determine which niches are popular, which are profitable and which aren't. You'll also want to see which markets are flooded with books and if you can carve out topics not being properly represented.

4. Become An Authority - Once you find some success in a niche try and build some more books around similar topics and become an authority on the subject. Not only will you look better in the eyes of readers resulting in more purchases but it will allow you to market multiple books to people you've already sold to and know are interested in your topic.

5. Create An Author Central Profile – This is a good place to let readers know a little about yourself or your pen name. It also collects all your books published under that name in one place so people who bought previous items can see if any of your other titles interest them.

6. Build A Back End - Use your books to bring people into your email list. This way you can market to them in the future and make them potential customers for years to come. You can also do things like build out a website revolving around products that benefit the people in your books niche. Drive people to your books through social media sites. There are a lot of possibilities. This is more of an advanced step. I would suggest getting some books published and making money before jumping into building your brand and back end.

Two good paid services for Kindle publishing that I use:

1. KBook Promotions
2, Kindle Spy

There might be other services on the market that are great but the two above are the only ones I have any experience with. I would suggest holding off on spending any money on extras like these until you've got a few books published and are sure it's a business you want to dive into and grow.

Marketing your Kindle book will help to drive sales and improve your rank in Amazon. Down below are some of the ways I market my books for free without having to go out and pay for promotion..

Every 90 days Kindle allows you to either run a Kindle Countdown Deal or 5 days of Free Book Promotion. You can divvy up the five days however you'd like. Personally I like to run 2 days, then a month later run 2 days, and finally towards the end of the 90 days run a 1 day promotion.

Join Goodreads with a regular account and then fill out your profile and upgrade for free to their Author Program. Once you've been upgraded (it can take a few days) you'll be able to write blogs, share book excerpts, write a quiz about your book, and notify followers of upcoming things.

Create social bookmarking accounts on Digg / StumbleUpon, Reedit and Delicious.

Create a Facebook page / Twitter account / Pinterest account / LinkedIn account / Instagram account for each page. Fill out the profiles and link to your website or Author central account on Amazon. Also be sure to add your books to each of the sites. Either by creating a board dedicated to your books on Pinterest or taking pictures regarding your book or something in your niche and putting them on Instagram.

Join as many Facebook Amazon Kindle / Free Book Promotion groups as you can find.

I also like to create a website dedicated to each pen name. It acts as a central hub for all my social media sites, home to my blog, a place to bring visitors to sign up for my email list, as well as place where all my books can be found.

Once all of your accounts have been created, you need to begin adding content and bringing in visitors. For my website I try and write a few short blog post each week. I also comment on niche relevant forums and websites linking back to my site.

When it comes to social media:

Social Bookmarking – When my books come out I post my links and website to StumbleUpon, Reedit, Digg, and Delicious

Twitter - I tweet a few times daily and follow people relevant in my niche. I also add links to my blog posts and other valuable content.

LinkedIn - I network and cross promote all my other social media accounts.

Pinterest - I add a few boards weekly revolving around my niche. I also an opt in to an Pinterest board and add pins to niche specific Pinterest boards,.

Instagram – I add niche specific photos or photos of my books. I also try and add other interesting pictures in order to draw a larger following.

Goodreads – Interact on the site, create quizzes, write reviews or add my blog posts.

I also promote each of my books using sites off this interactive list of book promotions site called Readers In The Know.

When running a Free Book Promotion I immediately post a link to my book on every Facebook group I'm member of, along with all my social media sites and my website. I the link I mention how long the book is on promo for and I ask anyone who wants to do an honest review swap and has a book on free promo to contact me. I also try and contact as many people as I can on my Facebook groups offering review swaps.

Here are a few Twitter users who will re-tweet your free book posts. Just include @ and their user name to tag them:

@kindleebooks
@DigitalBkToday
@Kindlestuff
@4FreeKindleBook
@KindleEbooksUK
@KindleFreeBook
@KindleBookKing
@FreeReadFeed

When doing review swaps I always flip through each of the pages and try and get a sense of the book. Be sure not to post your review right away. Amazon doesn't seem to like it. A good rule of thumb is to wait 5-7 days after you've gone through the book to post your review.

Personally, I don't hire this job out as I find it an easy enough process and like to save the extra money. It also allows me to see how other peoples books are put together and it has given me quite a few book ideas for profitable niches that I wouldn't have thought of otherwise.

** In general, each day I spend a few minutes or so marketing or adding value on each of these above sites under each of my different pen names. Whether it's writing blog posts, adding a status update, announcing a new book, marketing a free promotion or giveaway I find if you do a little bit every day you're less likely to get overwhelmed

** If you like to make videos then be sure to utilize YouTube to promote your books. I don't love being on camera so I prefer not to use this method for Kindle but I know plenty who do that have great results.

Twitter

This is one of my favorite tools I've used over the past few years to earn some extra money! If you're new to the Internet or haven't heard of Twitter before, it's a social marketing platform where you can "tweet" out messages of 140 characters or less to all of your followers. You can use this for any number of reasons from personal to professional. I'm going to focus on a few of the ways someone like you can use Twitter to begin making money online.

Create a Twitter account - Go to Twitter and sign up. Be sure to fill out your profile, add a picture and add a link to any product or page you choose to promote. This can be anything from a personal page to a Click Bank product to your online business. Don't worry I'll get more into this later.

Sign up for these sites - Why? Because these sites allow you to send out ads on your Twitter account and pay you money for the right to send out the ad or pay you for how many clicks the ad gets. Each site varies a bit so you'll have to read each site carefully and learn their policies and payout procedures.

1. Speakr
2. MyLikes
3. Sponsored Tweets

These sites won't break the bank in earnings but each can earn you a few extra bucks a month with minimal effort on your part. Remember every dollar counts and the more you make the more you'll have to grow your business.

One other suggestion for how to monetize your Twitter account is through sites like Click Bank. If you've never heard of Click Bank before it's a massive marketplace where you can sell your own information products or become an affiliate and sell another person's information products.

All you need to do is register for your free Click Bank account. After that's completed enter the Click Bank marketplace and choose a product you want to promote. You'll see some stats down at the bottom. One of those stats is called "Gravity". Be sure to look for products with high gravity scores as these products are the ones that are selling.

Next click on the Promote link and you'll be brought to a screen with your user name and the option to use a tracking code. I've never had the need to use a tracking code so I just leave that field blank and hit the "create" button. I'm then brought to a screen where I'm given an affiliate code to use. Now all you have to do is send out the occasional tweet advertising this product with your affiliate link.

One thing I want to mention. Be sure not to only send out ads on your Twitter account. The more personal you get and the more you engage your followers the better received the offers you do send out will be. Try to send out 60 to 100 regular tweets to every tweet suggesting a product you promote.

Facebook Pages

Facebook is home to over a billion registered users. This makes it an incredibly powerful and profitable tool to have at your disposal. I just want to touch on a few basic ways to earn some money using Facebook. In all honesty there's a ton of advanced techniques out there big enough to build an entire course around. This book is just trying to teach you how to use Facebook as an extra revenue stream not your main revenue stream.

1Build Facebook Pages around a Product or Service - One great way of bringing in some cash is to build pages around products or services. For example, you can go on Click Bank or a CPA site and find something to promote. Once you've found one that you're interested in, go here and create a Facebook page around it. After your page is all set up I would add a description, a few photos, opt in page to gather visitors emails (I prefer Aweber), CPA offer or affiliate links.

Here is a list of some Click Bank alternatives:

1. **Rakuten Linkshare**
2. **PayDotCom**
3. **ShareASale**

Here is a list of some CPA sites you can use:

1. **CJ**
2. **Cpalead**
3. **Peerfly**
4. **OfferVault**
5. **Fluxads**
6. **Maxbounty**
7. **Revenue Ads**

Now go to a site like Fiverr and type in "Facebook Fan Page". You'll find many people willing to invite thousands of their friends to your page for only $5.

Another great option is to go to Microworkers or Amazon Mechanical Turk and create a task for people to go and "like" your page. In this case I prefer using Amazon Mechanical Turk as I can get more "likes" for my page at a lower cost. By following the steps above you're page will begin to gain a large following eventually hitting a tipping point. When it hits this tipping point your page will begin to take off virally and that's where the real money begins. Be sure to stay active on your page and engage your followers. The more you do this the more you'll profit in the long run.

If you decide to use a CPA offer I've found that the ones that work best with Facebook Fan Pages are the simple submit offers. These offers only require you to fill out a short form and they pay anywhere from $2 to $3. When using Click Bank offers be sure to promote products that have a well put together landing page. There's no sense driving traffic to the offer if the landing page can't convert them. Remember to look for products with high gravity.

Flip Your Fan Page for Profits

Another technique I've used in the past is taking a successful Fan Page and building a basic Word Press site around it. You'll want to create a site with around 5 to 7 articles on it and have it link back directly to your Fan Page. Once you've got your new site up and running you can head over to a site like Flippa and sell your site for a profit. Be sure to advertise how successful your Fan Page is and what it is earning. This will ensure you get top dollar for your site. I'll go into more detail on flipping websites later on in this course but I wanted to share this particular technique I've used in the past.

There are a lot of ways to use Facebook to your advantage. If you already have a website you can use it to draw visitors and sell your products. You can also advertise a product or service using Facebook ads. Those are just a couple of further examples of how you can harness the power of Facebook and start making a profit.

YouTube

YouTube is another powerful social media tool you can use to make some cash. There a many ways to make money using this platform. Some you can get started on today and some you'll need to begin slowly building a solid foundation before starting. If you consider yourself to be creative and love to produce content then this might be the perfect place for you.

Tools for making YouTube videos

Video Camera / Web Cam / Some other kind of video recording device

Video editing software

* There are a lot of great free video editing software programs and paid video editing programs with more advanced features available. Go with whatever works best for you and your situation.

1. Become a part of YouTube's Partner Program. This first one is a big money maker but will take time and effort on your part. This is not one that will pay off right away but it has the most potential. People are making hundreds of thousands of dollars a year doing this. There are quite a few prerequisites for getting accepted into this program which is why it will take some time but I wanted to share it with you because it may be something worth pursuing. For instance you'll need to start uploading original content that you are allowed to monetize and you'll need to receive thousands of views on it. Once that has happened feel free to apply and if you get accepted you'll receive a ton of cool benefits. Some of those benefits include being able to monetize your videos, share in revenue produced from rentals and overlay ads, higher quality video, Insight analytic and branded channel options to name a few.

2. Become a part of YouTube Individual Video Partnerships. This is much like the first example except instead of aiming at users who upload a lot of content that gets views these partnerships center around an individual video that has taken off. If you create a video that goes viral or gets a bunch of views you may be able to partner up with YouTube and monetize it.

3. Find the latest popular videos and check to see if the owner is advertising at all or has a link in their description. Underneath where the video plays is where you would like to see if it's been advertised and over to the right are the suggested videos which I'll discuss in the next tip. With this technique you're searching for videos that don't have any links or advertising. Many people have wildly successful videos but never think of doing any advertising on them. You'll want to email these video owners and make them an offer to include your link on their description page. Do not offer a price in your first email keep it simple and see if they're willing to make a deal. If they are then you can negotiate. Once you've come to an agreement you can use CPA offers or head over to Click Bank and look for a product that revolves around the same keywords this video is targeting. If there are multiple products pick the one that looks the most professional and has the highest gravity. From here you'll want to register a cheap domain (.info domains are good) that's related to the niche and forward your site to the Click Bank or CPA offer.

** You can also try Fiverr and type in YouTube link. Many people are there offering to put your link on their video but be careful. You want to place your link on videos that get high volumes of traffic.

4. Another technique is to find popular videos and make a similar video targeting the same keywords and tags being used. This can help generate lots of views to your video because your video comes up in the suggested video section of the more popular videos. Now all you need to do is make sure your video has a link in the description to a product or CPA offer and you're off to the races.

5. Build a loyal audience and sell them your own products, courses or books. Selling to people directly over YouTube is a big business. Videos build trust and people feel more engaged and connected to you when they get a sense of who you are as a person and what you can offer them. Another great thing about this type of selling is you can engage your customers directly as little or often as you'd like with the help of Google Hangouts. Just go live and let people directly ask you questions or speak to you on video chat personally during the actual Hangout.

6. Make product review videos. Find an offer on one of the CPA sites above and make a review around the offer. You'll want to make sure the keywords for the product your reviewing have low competition and are something you can rank for in Google and YouTube. Once that is done upload the finished video to YouTube and begin promoting.

When making these types of review videos you can either use the talking head method or screen capture method. The talking head method is where you're in front of the camera yourself promoting the product and giving your review. The screen capture method is where you visually demonstrating your product while reviewing it.

The second requires a little more effort and some extra video presentation tools like Camtasia or Prezi. These tools aren't free but are worth the expense if you plan on making lots of videos.

Be sure to include a "Special Bonus" to help convert more visitors. It will serve two purposes. One it will get more people to buy your product and two it will get more people on your email list. The bonus can be anything from an e-book to a short audio course.

Make sure your video has a "Call To Action" telling people to act. You want to make sure you write a good exact keyword title. Videos should be short and sweet. Around The 5-8 minute mark is a good time to aim for. You also want to look at your top competitors videos, see what tags their using to get their video ranked, and then use those tags in your video.

** A few notes on the YouTube partner program listed above. Be sure to read through all their policies and requirements before applying if you apply and get rejected you'll have to wait 2 months till you can apply again. If you get accepted you'll need a Google AdSense account and be aware YouTube will only pay you once your video makes a certain amount. Also with the individual video partnerships YouTube will send you an email asking if you want to apply for revenue sharing regarding a specific video. If you get approved you can only monetize that video. YouTube is always updating there terms of service so be sure to check them over occasionally as these things sometime get tweaked and changed.

Some other sites to check out for opportunities include:

I use some of these sites for my Kindle business but I would not consider myself an expert in them. If you already use these platforms it might be something worth researching further.

1. **Instagram**
2. **Pinterest**
3. **Periscope**
4. **LinkedIn**

Stage #3 - Build It And They Will Come!

By this point you should have numerous revenue streams up and running. This is where you're going to want to start reinvesting some of the money you've earned and really begin to expand your online empire.

Stage #3 Goals

This is stage represents one of the cornerstones of your online empire. These techniques will passively make you money for years to come once they've been implemented. Many people stop after Stage # 3 because there already successful and either don't desire to make more or don't know how. In this stage you decide on your own goals. The goal I set for myself in this stage was to have a portfolio of 100 AdSense and Niche sites in a year. While you may think that number is high you need to remember I wasn't intent on doing this alone. I worked the previous stages extensively so I could outsource a lot of the work.

Whatever goal you decide is right for you make sure to take action and start working towards it. Even if it's only a little bit each day you'll see the results start to add up!

One of the ways to expand our online business is by creating a portfolio of two distinct types of websites:

1. AdSense sites
2. Niche sites

The great thing about these sites are that there is an unlimited amount of sites you can create and an equally unlimited amount of money you can earn. You can create only a handful of sites or manage a portfolio numbering in the hundreds to thousands. If all of your sites only earned a few dollars every month those dollars will quickly add up by building more sites.

I'm going to show you how to create these sites and teach you all the tips and tricks I've learned over the years that have helped make me a lot of money.

Here a links to a few sites and tools you'll be using when building these sites:

Google Keyword Planner - This tool is a good FREE option! It will help you narrow down the keywords you want to build your site around.

Long Tail Pro – This is a paid service but hands down my favorite. Easily trumps the FREE tools available. The $97 one time fee is the tier I personally use.

Google Analytics - Track how your website is performing. Take the time to learn Analytics it will pay off in the long run.

NameCheap - This is where I purchase my domains. Feel free to use any domain name company you prefer.

HostGator - This is my hosting company of choice. Feel free to use any hosting company you prefer.

AWeber – Grow your business with this email marketing tool. This is a paid service with different price tiers for different levels of use.

GetResponse – The alternative to Aweber.

AdSense Websites

Google AdSense sites are small 5-7 page websites built around a product where you're main source of income comes from Google AdSense. Google AdSense is an advertising platform that delivers text-based Google AdWords ads that are relevant to your site content pages. All you need to do is sign up for an AdSense account and once your application is approved you'll be able to create an ad block that you'll then place on your website using a snippet of code that Google provides you with. Once you've gone ahead and placed the ad block on your site it could take a few days before the ad block becomes targeted to your sites content. For example, if your website is about "puppies" your AdSense ad blocks will show ads relating to anything about puppies. This means when people visit your site they'll often click on these ads because they're interested in products or services relating to puppies. When someone clicks your ad you'll then earn money from Google. The amount you make per click will vary depending on how competitive the keyword you're targeting is.

** Be very careful to follow their Terms Of Service. If they suspect you of trying to game their system they will ban you forever.**

Finding A Product

This is easier than it sounds. New products flood the market each and every day. You'll learn that there is an endless amount of products ready to promote. When you get right to it you'll find that you'll have the most success with AdSense sites when you create product based sites to revolve around a specific product, product type or product line.
You'll want to base your site around a specific product, product type or product line. The reasons you want to do this are you'll get a higher CTR on your AdSense ads, it's easy to rank in Google for exact match domains, and it's easy to write content around these types of sites.

1. What you need to do is head over to a site like Amazon Bestsellers. Amazon is the largest retailer of physical products on the Internet. You'll be able to find tons of great ideas here to help get you started..

2. Choose a section from the main page or from the list of categories on the left hand side. For this example I chose the bestseller category Kitchen & Dining on the left hand side of the page

3. The bestsellers change every day but scroll down your page and you might still see EatSmart Precision Pro Digital Kitchen Scale. This looks like something I might be interested in building a site around.

4. At this point I want to get a piece of paper and a pen. I then write down the name of this product in this instance "EatSmart Precision Pro Digital Kitchen Scale".

5. Now I'm going to repeat the previous 4 steps and find 15 different products I want to explore further.

Keyword Research

This is a key component to creating a successful AdSense site. If you do this step wrong then it will limit the amount of money you'll make. Doing proper keyword research is the most important part of building a successful AdSense site!

When do this step correctly SEO becomes easy! You'll be able to build a stream of sites that get good traffic and earn you money! Any time you decide you need more traffic to your site just target a new keyword and watch the visitors come in.

Here are the three important factors in finding top notch keywords:

1. Monthly Search Volume
2. Cost Per Click (CPC)
3. Number Of AdWords Advertisers

Let's break each of these down and I'll discuss why each one is important.

Monthly Search Volume – This is the number of people who visit a given keyword on a monthly basis. Your ideal keyword has a high monthly search volume. More searches equals more traffic which equals more money. I've seen that roughly around 1000 searches = $20 dollars in revenue on the sites we're going to create. When picking a keyword for your site try not to go under 500 – 600 searches a month. This is really the bare minimum!

Cost Per Click (CPC) – This is the amount an advertiser pays Google whenever someone searches a certain keyword and clicks on the advertisers ad. Since we split this revenue with Google (they don't give us an exact number on the % shared) the higher the CPC the more money we stand to make. Your ideal keyword has a CPC of $.50 cents or higher. You'll generally average half that amount after Google takes their cut. You can go as low as $.25 cents but I wouldn't make it a habit.

Number Of AdWords Advertisers – This is the number of AdWords advertisers that are bidding on a keyword. Your ideal keyword has a bunch of advertisers. I would aim for at least 10 advertisers for a given keyword although I would go as low as 5 or 6. A couple of great ways to find the number of advertisers for a given keyword is to:

a.) Type the keyword into Google and count the number of advertisers up top and too the right.

b.) Use a great site called SpyFu. This has a paid service they promote but what I'm going to use it for is **FREE**. Just enter your given keyword into the box where it says enter your domain or keyword and then hit search. This will bring you to a new screen that lists a bunch of information about the keyword. For our purposes I want to focus on the average CPC along with the number of advertisers. I want to mention that not every keyword will bring back search results especially some of the more specific products. When this occurs you should just use the first step to determine the amount of advertisers.
Personally I always use both steps. SpyFu is great but sometimes I find more advertisers listed on Google then SpyFu shows.
On the next page I've used a generic example using the keyword "dog training tips" to give you an example of what the results would look like. When I pull it up it lists the CPC as being $2.27 - $2.79 and it shows 3 advertisers

In summary your ideal keyword should meet the guidelines I've listed above. If it doesn't meet all the qualifications then it's time to move on and use a different keyword. This is one of the reasons I had you find 15 different products. Now you can weed out the keywords that aren't profitable and find the best keyword from the ones that are.

How To Perform Keyword Research

There are many tools available to help you with your keyword research. Market Samurai is a popular one although I have no personal experience with it. I personally use Long Tail Pro which is an excellent keyword tool.

If you don't want to shell out the money for a good keyword tool you can do a lot of the heavy lifting for free. I would suggest getting one in the near future. Do some research and find a tool that you're comfortable with. In the long run it's going to not only save you a lot of time and energy automating many of the tasks I'm going to share with you but it's also going to help you find a ton of extra profitable keywords.

Step 1 - Open up the Google AdWords Keyword Tool. Once you're there sign up for free or sign into your Google AdWords account. The sign in button is at your top right of the screen. You can use this tool without signing in but it will pull back fewer results (about 100) and won't include all the data (CPC).

Step 2 - Once you've signed in click on "Find New Keyword" and type your keyword into the "word or phrase" field and click the blue "Get Ideas" button. For this example will use the keyword "EatSmart".
As you can see Google has pulled back all the terms related to "EatSmart". Remember we're looking for exact match results.
When I pulled up the keyword "EatSmart" it shows that it currently gets 1900 global monthly searches. Unfortunately only one of the other keywords listed below it got above the minimum. You could still use this site if the domain for "EatSmart" was available and it met all the other criteria but in this instance all three of the "EatSmart" domain names had been taken. At this juncture we would cross this one off of our list and move on to the next keyword.

*** If you run into an occasion where you find a really great main keyword but no real additional keywords you can decide to continue on to the next step. Although I don't personally do so I know many people who make 1 or 2 page AdSense sites instead of the larger ones that I focus on. Neither is wrong it's more of a personal preference on my part.

For checking domains I use a keyword tool. If you don't have a keyword tool that can do this automatically I would suggest going over to a domain registrar like NameCheap and looking to see if any of the domains for whatever keyword you're searching for are still available. It may take you a few tries to find one that still has domains available but there are plenty of them out there and new products get released every day creating even more opportunity. Once you do find one with an available domain name head over to Google and do a little more research.

Remember Google ranks each of your pages so every page needs to target a different keyword that is related to your product. Don't target keywords that are off topic as this will hurt those pages rankings.

Example:

If your site targets Barska rifle scopes then your keywords could target a specific type of rifle scope like a Barska tactical rifle scope. What you don't want to do is have a site about Barska rifle scopes that targets a keyword like puppies. Another thing you don't want to do is target a keyword that shares the same brand but a different function. For instance Barska rifle scopes and Barska safes are two completely different topics. Even though they're both Barska related their not specific to the same type of product which in this case is rifle scopes.

Content and Website Launch

Before building a site and adding content you need to choose a domain name. It is very important that you use an exact match domain name when building these sites. For example the main keyword of http://www.EatSmartScale.com is Eat Smart Scale. If the .com of your main keyword is taken it is fine to use a .net or .org variation. Do not use any other extensions besides these three. Having a .com is the best option but if you can't get it I would try an .org extension first then a .net extension.

If you don't have a keyword tool that will automate this step for you then go to your domain provider and begin searching for the exact match domains for the main keyword you've targeted. Many of these will be taken but you'll be able to find more than a few available. This is another reason why it's important to have a list of 15 or so different products to choose from. The more options you give yourself the easier time you'll have finding domains.

Once you've found a domain name that you're happy with then go ahead and register it. At this point you'll want to sign up for a hosting account if you don't already have one. I would recommend HostGator but any hosting company you're happy with is fine.

Next you'll want to create your site and add your main page and articles targeting around 3 to 5 additional keywords. This will help to bring in additional traffic and make you more money. If your search volume is high enough on your main keyword you can make less additional articles I'll leave that up to you. Personally I always make 3 to 5 more. It doesn't take a long time upfront and it will pay off for you in the long run.

Having your site optimized correctly can make all the difference. You want to draw the visitor's eyes towards your AdSense ads and boost your click through ratio (CTR) as high as possible. The more clicks you get the more money you make!

Here are a few things you I want to share with you before you create your own site.

1. These sites can be basic no frills sites... In fact, these sites work best when you keep things simple. If you follow that logic you're going to have a lot of success with your AdSense sites.

2. Unique Content - Don't copy content or use spinners when creating content for these sites. Google does not like this and it will lower your search engine rankings. I would also make your article between 800 - 1500 words. It needs to be reasonably well written and all spelling and grammar errors should be corrected.

3. Creating content for product sites is easy. Just go to the products main site and do a little research. Write some general information about the company producing the product, some general information about the product itself, the benefits and uses of the product, and why the customer should buy the product. Once you get into a rhythm you'll be churning out a new article every 45 minutes to an hour.

4. Make sure your sites incorporate these three Meta tags for each page on your site that is targeting a keyword: A title tag, a description tag and a keyword tag. These tags are important because they tell the search engines what keywords to rank you for. So if the keyword for your page is "EatSmart" then both the title and keyword tag would be EatSmart while the description would be just that. A brief description of your site that incorporates your keyword.

Take this description for example:

"EatSmart Products is a leading manufacturer and distributor of bathroom scales, kitchen scales, food scales and luggage scales."

5. Have a relevant picture at the top of each of your pages just above your title with your Google AdSense ad right underneath it. I have found that doing this will dramatically increase your click through ratio (CTR). You can get these images from a variety of places including the website where the product is sold. I've never had a problem doing this as your site is promoting their company and driving traffic to their products.

6. Make sure to keep the text on your website gray and not black. This is going to help blend our text with the AdSense ads. Just another way to boost your CTR.

7. If you haven't already signed up for Google AdSense make sure you go and do that now. After you've been accepted go into your account and click the "My Ads" tab on the top left side of the page. Then click on the "New Ads" button and follow this formula for creating your AdSense ads: Make sure that the background color is white to blend in with the background of your page. Make sure that the link text is blue. Make sure that the size of the ad block is 336 X 280. Make sure that the ad is placed just below the title. Make sure that you only use one AdSense block per page. Make sure you're only using text based ads. Once you're done creating your ad Google will give you a snippet of code to add to your site. Go back to your hosting and ad this snippet to each page you're targeting a keyword on. Pretty soon you're ads will be up and running.

8. For the title of each of my additional keyword pages I only use the keyword itself so if the keyword were "EatSmart Digital Scale" that would be the title of my page.

9. I use WordPress on a lot of my sites. I personally like the features and flexibility but feel free to use a different one of your choosing.

10. Hold back one or two of your articles and wait a few days to add each of them to your site. The reason behind this is that Google loves new content. This will show Google that you're keeping your site fresh and updated and will help to boost your rankings.

11. Before you're finished with your site you should go to Google Analytics and sign your site up for tracking. They have detailed instructions on how to do this there but basically you'll be given another snippet of code to place on your site. Having Google Analytics will not only help you track a ton of information about your customer base it will be helpful to have in case you ever decide to sell your site for a profit at a later date.

Getting Traffic

I use a variety of ways to drive traffic to my site. Here a few of the methods I use.

1. I'm a big fan of article marketing. Even if you don't like this method you should submit at least a few articles to Ezine Articles. This by far the most popular article marketing site and can drive lots of your traffic to your site. Follow the same tips for writing these articles as you would an article for your site. The main difference is that you'll often be allowed to add 1or 2 links in either the body of the article or in an author's box at the end of the article. Target your keywords for the page you're linking to through the use of anchor text. So if the keyword you're targeting is "EatSmart" and your domain you were linking to was EatSmart.com then the HTML code you would use to create the anchor text looks like this:

<a href="http://www.eatsmart.com">EatSmart</a>

2. Promote your site on social media. Take advantage of Twitter, Instagram, Facebook groups and YouTube to plug your site and drive traffic.

3. Write a short eBook driving traffic to an email list or website. Give it away for FREE on social media or upload it to Amazon Kindle and run a free promotion giving it away.

4. I also submit my sites to between 10-20 free directories. This is a great way to get some initial links and start getting those Google spiders to begin indexing your pages. Visit this site Directory Critic for an updated list of thousands of directories. I like to start in the new section because I know my link will get approved faster. I then submit to some more established directories for good measure.

5 I mix up each of these techniques for about 3 weeks. Try to spread this out evenly. Don't do everything in one day and then leave the site alone. Google likes its linking to be natural so try and do a little bit each day. After these 3 weeks my site is usually ranking pretty highly for my given keywords. Google is funny so sometimes I'll rank quicker than this and sometimes it will take nearly twice as long. Don't be surprised to see your site fluctuate in rankings dramatically at first. Over time your rankings will begin to stabilize. This is known as the Google Dance.

6. If you're still having problems ranking continue to add new content every few days or once a week. Google wants sites to provide fresh original content. Provide that and you're more likely to rank highly in the search engine results.

7. At this point I go into maintenance mode. Every month or so I spend a few more hours writing a couple more articles to either distribute or put on my site. I also do some extra back linking but that's about it. Otherwise I just sit back and wait for the money to start rolling in!

As you can see building AdSense sites is like finding gold! You can build an unlimited amount of sites and create unlimited amounts of wealth. I urge you to take action on the steps I've provided you. The best way to get started is by getting started. You may make some mistakes along the way but chalk those up to experience and try not to make them again. Before long you'll be a seasoned pro.

Niche Websites

Niche sites are great because like AdSense sites the topics you can choose from are limitless. For example, you can choose to build a site about dog training where you can sell either a product created by someone else (Click Bank) or your own dog training course.
These types of sites also allow you to use opt in forms like Aweber to build a list of loyal customers you can sell to over and over again for years to come.. Just offer them something of value for free and you'll convert like crazy.

These sites are considered to be "evergreen" because once they are set up and have attained some good rankings for your keywords you'll be able to make a passive income for years to come.

Choosing A Market

This is similar to the process used when choosing an AdSense site. I still do all the keyword research I did before only I no longer care as much about CPC or the amount of AdWords advertisers. .

The main difference is I can pick any topic not just one revolving around a product. Instead of using Google Trends or Amazon Bestsellers I use the entire web to help give me ideas. You can find inspiration for a topic anywhere. Choose something you're passionate about or something that you consider a hobby. The possibilities are endless. All you need to do is brainstorm for a few minutes and you'll have tons of ideas to research.

I would pick a few different niches to explore and go with the one that has the highest main keyword exact match monthly search volume and the additional keywords that also have high monthly search volume. If you find a niche with a lot of great potential keywords you've hit the jackpot. Now all you have to do is create the site, write some articles, drive some traffic, and cash out.

Domain and Hosting

This step hasn't changed. You still need to go to your domain registrar and buy your domain name and you still need to go to your hosting company and set up your website. I prefer using WordPress to build all my sites as it's rich with features but still easy to master.

Content

Let me first show you what a successful niche website looks like. You can either model your site around this one or take your chances and create a site of your own design. There are many ways to build a profitable niche site! I just wanted to show you an example of something that works. Like the AdSense sites your niche sites don't need to be fancy to get the job done.

http://www.BettaFishCenter.com

How you create content for a niche site is nearly identical to how you would create content for an AdSense site. Unique original content is a must! Don't use spinners to generate your content. Google will figure it out and punish you for it.

You still want your articles to be a minimum of 800 words. The longer your article is the better but as long as it's over 800 words you'll be fine.

Articles still need to be well written and proofed for grammar and spelling mistakes. Your site is trying to get people to opt in to a mailing list and buy products. The more professional your site appears the more money you'll make.

Some of main differences between AdSense sites and niche sites are that niche sites don't need to revolve around a product they can be about anything from gluten free diets to learning about how to become a magician. Another difference is that you won't be driving traffic to AdSense ads. Now you'll be driving traffic to your opt in or one of your products. The higher your pages opt in converts the more products you sell in the long run. Also while most AdSense sites are small only 3-5 pages your niche websites should be a minimum of 10-12 pages. I try to aim for 25 pages but for those just starting out 10-12 pages should do the trick.

Don't be afraid to add video to your site to make it stand out from other more basic sites. Simplicity will work just fine but the more you engage your visitors the more likely you are to turn them into customers.

Adding a small forum to your site may be another idea you want to explore

Remember you're setting these sites up to stand the test of time. If you put in a hundred percent when creating them it's going to reflect in the amount of money they generate. As you make more sites you'll find ways to streamline the process and cut down on the time it takes to finish them.

Eventually you can even go to sites like Upwork and Elance and pay to have the most time consuming work outsourced in order to get more sites built quickly.

Building Your List and Opt In Page

Your list equals money. Many people don't realize the power of a having a large and responsive mailing list. There are quite a few millionaires out there just because they took the time to cultivate and properly maintain their list.

Everyone who is on your list is not only a potential customer today but a potential customer for years to come.

First you need to get an Aweber account or another auto responder account if you don't already have one. For our purposes I'm going to refer to Aweber since that is the company I use.

What is an auto responder?

An auto responder is a type of email system that can automatically mail out information to the individuals who decide to sign up. The information you can send ranges from e-newsletters, one time offers, daily tips, and special mini courses to offers promoting your products, general updates and important announcements. Whatever you use it for generally depends on the needs of your business.

What is An Opt-In Box?

An Opt in box is a small box on your web page where you can have people put their information which will go into the auto responder such as their name and email address. If you use Aweber you will find plenty of tutorials on their site that will walk you through how easy the process is of placing one on your website. This might sound daunting at first but it really is a simple process once you've done it a few times.

Once They Subscribe, Now What?

1. Value, Value, Value!

You need to give people a reason to subscribe to your opt in list. People are getting more and more wary about handing out their personal emails. Nowadays, you need to offer as much value as possible, in order to entice them into signing up. Whether you're offering a special 10 part mini course on something related to your niche, a special PDF e-Book, a webinar or series of instructional videos it doesn't matter. What does matter is that whatever you're offering contains value and benefits the subscriber in some fashion.

2. Continually write follow-up emails!

Now that you have your opt in page set up offering your special 10 part course, interview recording, PDF e-Book (or whatever you come up with of value) it's time to begin writing email follow-ups on a regular basis.

These email follow-ups are your way to connect with potential customers. The goals of these follow-ups are to let people know more about you, build trust, get them to like you, and hopefully to start buying from you.

One of the best techniques to use is to tell people stories from your own life. Then take those stories and tie them into whatever product you happen to be promoting. By sharing personal parts of your life, people, will naturally begin to connect with what you're saying. This won't all happen in the course of one or two emails but over time it will. That's the reason why it's so important to maintain regular contact with the people who subscribe to you through email.

Having an auto responder like Aweber allows you to write a ton of these emails at once and paste them into their system. At that point you can have emails sent out every day, every week or on whatever time frame you choose. This system will also manage your list and has a ton of other options and features.

Writing follow up emails is a process that never ends on a great email list. Don't just send out emails promoting things. You want to send out emails with a lot of value and then occasionally send out an email promoting a product that you've either created or are an affiliate of. When sending out affiliate offers you need to be sure to only send out emails about quality products. You don't want to lose the trust you've worked so hard to build over another person's shoddy product. That's a surefire way to have people unsubscribe from your list.

3. Drive traffic to your Site!

This is where the real marketing begins. You need to set aside a portion of time each day to start driving traffic to your site.

Here are a few quick and easy ways to get going:

A) Look for forums in the niche your promoting. Join these forums and start contributing. By helping out others you're only helping yourself. Be sure to advertise your site in your signature file. Using forums can be an excellent way of establishing yourself as an expert.

B) Find blogs on the niche you're promoting and add helpful comments. Just like with the forums you need to get involved in the conversations going on in your niche. Be sure to post on these blogs regularly. This will not only further establish your reputation it could grab the attention of the blog owner and open up the possibility of future joint venture projects.

C) Write and submit articles to article directories. Writing quality articles are one of the best long-term strategies of driving traffic to you page. There's one Internet marketer I know of who wrote 1,000's of articles during the course of a 12 month period, each article he wrote sent individuals to his one of his pages. He never used any other methods of driving traffic and he gets ton of visitors daily because of his hard work and focus in just one area of marketing. Of course this won't be for everyone but I just wanted to show you that these techniques will get results if you're willing to work them.

Here's a list of some of the top article directories to submit your articles to:

1. Ezinearticles
2. Articlesbase
3. Pubarticles
4. Buzzle
5. Goarticles
6. Sooperarticles
7. Ezinemark

Another good alternative place to promote articles:

1. Hubpages

Additional Tips, Methods and Strategies To Help You Build Your List.

1. Have a "Join My List" link somewhere in all your online content. If you have any articles on other websites or have a separate blog you need to include a way to join your list. All it takes is something simple. For example, "Like this article? Well you can have more like it delivered right to your inbox. Subscribe now for our monthly newsletter."

2. Have a "Join My List" link embedded in your signature file. If you're serious about building your list then you need to add a link to your list in all of your signature files. That means your email signature, the user profile signature on all the forums you use and in all your correspondence on social networking sites.

3. Run contests and give out prizes! Get creative. Give people a reason to sign up and they often will. You can hold these contests as often as you'd like. For example you can run a "Refer a Friend" contest and hold a monthly drawing for a prize.

4. Network and promote your list even when your offline. The more you get your name out there and push your list the quicker you're list is going to grow.

5. Create products and give affiliates 100% commission! This will make your product stand out from the rest and will get more affiliates to promote you. This won't make you money on the front end but that was never the point as it will add a ton of loyal buyers to your list and if they bought from you once it'll be much easier to sell to them again.

6. Create social media accounts to promote your site. Things like Facebook Fan Pages and Twitter accounts can go a long way in driving traffic to your site and opt-in box while also in building trust with your followers.

Launching Your Site

Before launching make sure you're all links work (Google hates broken links). Make sure all your pages are formatted properly and they're free of spelling and grammar errors.

You also want to be sure that you've targeted all your keywords and added your Meta tags (use the same process as the AdSense sites) to each page.

Have all your graphics and photos added and formatted. You don't want your presentation of the site to be sloppy. Don't know how to create graphics? That's fine just go to sites like Elance and Upwork. If it's something small go to a site like Fiverr or Gigbucks and have someone create them for you.

Don't forget to add your opt in page and free auto responder series for subscribers.

Write at least four additional articles that you haven't uploaded to your site. Every 7 days upload one new article. Google loves updated content and this help will boost your rankings.

I follow the same traffic plan for my niche sites that I do for my AdSense sites. The only difference is that instead of 3 weeks I spend closer to 6 weeks of steady promotion. You don't have to do a lot each day but Google likes to see natural linking. I also add a new article to my site every week which also gives me an added boost with Google.

My advice is to never stop adding these sites. Once you get to a certain point you may want to even consider outsourcing all of your main tasks to save you time. If outsourcing is something you want to learn more about then I would highly recommend John Jonas Replace Myself. It's a membership site that will teach you how to outsource your business and do it inexpensively.

There are a ton of other methods out there to explore once these sites are up and running from things like Gmail marketing techniques to using sites such as LinkedIn to build your business. I don't have a lot of experience in these areas but I just wanted to show you there are many different additional avenues you can explore once your current sites are earning you a healthy passive income each month.

** Don't be afraid to change things up and adapt with the times. What works now won't work forever. The internet is constantly evolving, and new ways of marketing are always being created. If you're able to stay ahead of the curve when it comes to marketing you'll be in a highly advantageous position.

Stage #4 - Expand Your Horizons!

At this point your business is really taking off. You should have a nice portfolio of AdSense and Niche websites generating a nice chunk of change for you each and every month. Be sure to keep an eye on each of these sites and if one of them ever starts to suffer, do a little SEO and add an article or two. Remember each article you add targets a new profitable keyword so this will only further increase your earnings over time.

If you're ready then these are a few things that can take your online business to the next level. Some of these are harder to accomplish than others. Don't get intimidated. If you feel you're lacking a certain amount of expertise to pull some of these things off there are plenty of resources available online to help you. Not only that but there are sites specifically aimed at helping you find and hire people to perform tasks you need done but don't either have the time or experience to accomplish. Two of these sites are Elance and Upwork. I suggest you go check them out if you ever get stuck or are looking to build a team of workers. You can find talented people to do anything from writing articles to programming entire websites.

Stage #4 Goal

At this point of the game you have one of two options. First you can just continue building your eBay & Amazon business, Kindle Publishing business, as well as your AdSense and niche websites. The second option is you can begin to find new methods and sources of revenue to further build your online empire.

For many people this first option is what their most comfortable with and that's perfectly acceptable. There's unlimited growth potential for these types of businesses so sticking to building them will work out just fine. For the rest of you now is where things get interesting. There are many different new avenues to explore. I would start with the first one I've mentioned below as it's the easiest to get started with and presents the least amount of risk in my opinion.

Before starting with any of these ventures do your research and find out as much information about each as you can. The more knowledge you have going in the less your mistakes will potentially cost you. For example, with flipping websites for profit you'll want to research the different places to sell and buy? How much if anything they charge for listing fees? What sites get the most traffic? Having these answers will only help you down the road.

Flip Websites For Profit

This is an excellent way to make big profits quickly. Sites like Flippa and Digital Points Forum allow you to sell or buy websites easier than ever before. You'll want to go to each of these sites and read there rules, procedures and pricing structure before getting started. Flippa is the biggest and most well known place to flip sites followed by Digital Points Forum but there are a bunch of other places you can do this. Honestly I could build a whole course around this and one day I might. For now I'll hit you with a few key things and basic concepts you should keep in mind. If you need more help then I would recommend doing further research. There's plenty of forums and places that can provide assistance.

Some key things to remembering when flipping websites.

1. You can create your own websites and flip them or buy other people's websites or mobile apps, retool them and sell them for a hefty profit. Whichever you choose be sure to follow the same steps you used above for creating your other sites. You can create either AdSense or niche sites the choice is up to you.

2. Always do your homework before purchasing any site. Make sure the owner provides you with things like the traffic stats over the last year, monthly and yearly earnings, what sources those earnings came from, and how the keywords being targeted are ranking in Google. Don't be afraid to speak up and ask questions! If you have something nagging you about a site then ask. The worse thing a seller can do is deny your request for information and at that point you kind of have your answer anyway.

3. **GIVE, GIVE, GIVE!** When selling a site add as much value for the buyer as you can. Look around Flippa and see what other sellers are offering or get creative and come up with some cool things yourself. Also have as much information possible to give to bidders. I see too many sellers watch their sites go unsold because they didn't do basic things like add Google Analytics to their site to check traffic. You want to make the buyers decision as easy as possible. Don't give them a chance to second guess things or talk themselves out of buying.

4. Answer any questions you get as thoroughly and as quickly as possible. Some bidders aren't willing to wait around for an answer. Stay on top of your auctions!

5. Never buy sites that don't have unique content! Google doesn't like duplicate content. Your rankings will suffer because of this! You should use Copyscape to check a site's content for originality.

6. Offer bonuses and extra content if they purchase your BIN (Buy It Now Price). You'll often get buyers ready to take a good site off the open market before competition heats up especially if they're getting added value for doing so.

Product Creation

Tired of selling other people's products? Want to take home a bigger slice of the profits? If so, then product creation might be just the thing for you. Boost your site's earnings by creating your own products to sell. Not only can you market them on your site but you can add them to sites like Click Bank or offer them as WSO's on the Warrior Forum.

Creating your own products will bring your business to the next level. If you're creating a mobile app then you can also sell you're item on both the Android and iTunes App Store. If you've created a course teaching people how to do something specific then you can use a platform like Udemy or Skillfeed to grow your business.

The great thing about product creation is you're only limited by your imagination. If you don't have time to create your own product you can always hire someone to help you. This is a great way to start building a brand and start gaining trust among consumers. Many people I know have parlayed a few successful product creations into a full out brand.

Many people get suckered into the belief that you need a great idea to be involved with product creation. This is **FLAT OUT NOT TRUE!** What most people don't realize is that many of the greatest products, no matter what the market, take existing ideas and present them in a better way.

If you can make a product or idea look better, easier to use, or more enjoyable then you've got the potential to earn money.

Don't get me wrong great ideas are a wonderful thing to have when creating a product there just not a necessity. There are actually three different easy methods you can use to create new products.

Method # 1 – Conflate

This method is where you take a few different methods and combine them into one information product. You'll want to improve upon these ideas or at least polish them up and simplify them if possible. Anything you can do to make your product stand out from the crowd!

Method #2 – Demonstrate

This method is where you take a product or concept you deem of value and create a video around it. Videos are the big thing in the information product market. People love watching things being explained.

Method #3 – Extrapolate

This method is where you take an interesting concept or idea and create an entire new in depth product about it. The great thing is this can be done on any subject or topic. For example if you like Twitter you could create an entire product based around Twitter and all the amazing things you can accomplish using it.

These three easy methods can be used individually or together when creating your products. The possibilities are endless!

Membership Sites

You're probably a seasoned Internet warrior at this stage of the game. Probably learned a few tricks, maybe even developed a few super secret ninja money making tactics of your own. If you've got something of value to offer the Internet community you might want to consider building a membership site. This is a big job that will require a lot of time, money, sweat and tears. However, the payoff can be enormous. I know quite a few people who have built million dollar businesses around membership sites.

If you're serious about pursuing this then I suggest you start doing your homework and make a detailed game plan of what your membership site is trying to accomplish. It might also be a smart idea to scout out your competition and join a few of their membership sites to see what they're doing and how you can improve upon it. You'll also want to begin making some contacts with the top Internet marketers in your field. These guys cross promote one another all the time and if you can get in with some of them you're business will explode.

11 Things To Know:

1. Preeminence – This is a vital part of any successful membership site! What is preeminence? Well, it means that people think you are the best, one of the best or at least better than other people, at what you do. It's due to preeminence that individuals pick your site over the competition, that you can have higher prices and why people come looking for you instead of you needing to find clients. This can be done by aligning yourself with other successful people in your field, being known for providing a ton of value in your area of expertise or getting coverage from media outlets. It may take a little time and persistence to accomplish these things but the extra work can pay big dividends.

2. Demonstrate Social Proof – Always provide an overabundance of value to people on your list or people visiting your site. Show them how you've succeeded up until this point and give them reasons why they should listen to you or sign up to your site for mentoring.

3. Branding Your Membership Site - Naming your product and coming up with the business image is so important in today's Internet marketplace. How does your site stand out from the thousands of other sites online? What's your hook? What's your message?

4. Triggers – You want people to feel a certain way when looking at your product in order to convince them to buy it. Evoking these triggers is an important part of any successful membership site. You want to "sell" people on you and your site by feeding into their needs and desires.

5. Content – Bill Gates once said "Content is King" Well in this case not only is content king but adding value is as equally important! If you want to keep members once there in the door you'll need to continually add new valuable content.

6. Reciprocity – Help others and they'll help you. Simple concept right! Membership sites are all about leveraging your connections with others to attain a larger customer base. If you have the opportunity to assist or help others in your field they'll likely be there to help you out when needed. Down the line maybe they'll post a guest blog or send out a sales letter to their email list about your site.

7. Website Creation - Figuring out the layout and features of your site is a crucial element. You can have the greatest content in the world but if it's hard to navigate your sight people won't stick around very long. Also how are you going to deliver your content? Do you plan on using audio, video, written guides, or a combination of all three? How are you going to secure the information on your site and handle payments?

8. Price Points - Too low and people won't take you seriously. Too high and you lose out on potential customers.

9. Always Offer a Guarantee - People want to feel like they have no risk by joining your site. If you show confidence in your site then people will feel confident about purchasing it.

10. Marketing and Advertising – How do you plan on announcing yourself to the world! Who are your customers and where do they normally hang out online? How are you going to promote the membership website? For example, are you going to use affiliates, if so what's there cut! You'll need to have answers for all these types of questions if you want to be successful

11. Traffic - Deciding on your SEO strategy for the site. Do you hire someone to handle it or do you handle it in house? This is just one of the many decisions you'll need to make. Do you know what a sales funnel is? If not, you might want to take the time to go out and learn.

Stage #5 - Eureka I've Reached The Promised Land!

Your online empire should be blowing up! From here on out the world is your oyster. If you're smart you'll begin to look for bigger and better opportunities to take your business to new heights. At this point your operation should be a well oiled machine. If you don't already have a team working for you to build new sites and help you in other areas expanding your business than you should get one. I'm not saying you need to hire a full staff but you should start having a few people handling a lot of the day to day activities leaving you to manage and handle the big picture.

Stage #5 Goal

Keep those money trains rolling down the tracks! Some people are searching for more no matter what they have in life. For some it's more money and for some it's the next challenge. You've spent awhile getting to this point and you've made a lot of money. My advice to you is to carefully assess risk before getting sucked into any big projects. Big rewards often come up with big costs up front and if those rewards don't materialize you can be left holding the bag.

Hopefully by this point you've grown a list of contacts and have been doing some networking. If you have or even if you haven't and you have a project you think can't miss you might want to try mitigating some of your risk through the use of partnerships, investors or funding sites like Kickstarter and Indiegogo. Using these platforms may lower the rewards but by sharing the risk you're protecting the money you have made and oftentimes that is a win in itself.

Product Launches

Product launches have become a big business online over the past few years. Properly positioning and marketing your product can lead to massive profits in minuscule amounts of time. Now I'm not talking about smaller products you would sell on Click Bank or Warrior Forum. I'm talking about full information product courses that many of the bigger names sell for upwards of a few thousand dollars. While smaller products can bring in big profits, for these product launches I'm talking about the big products that can bring in crazy amounts of money. If you've gotten to this final stage and you still hunger for new challenges and conquests then this is one more type of project to tackle.

Here a few thoughts and things for you to think about when deciding on how to properly launch a large new product into the marketplace.

1. Before you even think of beginning to market your product or get the word out your search engine optimization needs to be on point. You need to have a "home page" which is search friendly and user friendly. You might want to seriously think about producing a product specific landing page that has video, photos and descriptions all nicely laid out. This page needs to be coded correctly, complete with title tags, Meta tags, keyword rich text, header text and a unique URL that all properly reflect your new product

2. Depending on your product don't discount traditional media. I know that online new media gets all the hoopla surrounding it but television, radio and print media outreach is still an effective and often underutilized tool in exposing your product to the people. You need to have an effective and pointed campaign that clearly shows why your product is newsworthy, how it differs from other products, and the benefits you'll get from purchasing it. You can also take advantage of sites like Help a Reporter Out. Just one excellent resource for finding journalists in search of new story ideas and experts.

3. Don't forget about other proven marketing methods like trade shows, speaking engagements, direct mail, and promotional events. These might not be right for every product but you'd be foolish to ignore them if they could provide some benefit. With new products you can ill afford to waste any opportunities. You need to know the behaviors and the demographics of the customers you're aiming to reach. If you can't answer those questions you're not ready for market yet.

4. Online tools play a huge role in any successful product launch, especially those dealing with web based information products. Using tools like Google AdWords and some of the alternative pay per click (PPC) services will not only raise your products awareness but also funnel people right to the product. Advertising online allows you to target a specific audience but still cast a wide reach. You can also do some additional research and target the most popular blogs and websites used by those in the industry you're going after and advertise there. This is an amazing way to not only get your product seen but also to build solid relationships with some of the online movers and shakers. Last but certainly not least don't forget about advertising on social networks. Facebook ads are huge with billions of dollars in sales each year. Please no matter where you advertise make sure your ads are easily clickable and will direct any potential customers to a product specific landing page like I mentioned earlier.

5. Don't underestimate the power of a great email list! Email marketing is an excellent way to deliver new product information to people that you've already built solid relationships with in the past. Offer them early access or a special sneak peak at what your product can do. Maybe offer them a discount. There are many effective methods for getting these people to purchase your product.

6. Use the power of social networks to your advantage! Be sure to inform any brand enthusiasts along with any previous customers by getting your message out among your current social networks. Be sure to engage your audience and keep the conversation relevant. Most people nowadays are using some form of social network. You need to make your message stand out from all the other background noise. Get creative! Use things like photos, podcasts, contests, live chat and video to make you and your product stand out.

7. Target blogger and other social media influencers. Building relationships with these people can spread your message to more targeted people than many traditional outlets can. Always be respectful and helpful in return. The sword can cut both ways if you're not.

8. Don't forget about online retailers. Building good relationships with the big retailers of the world like Amazon and eBay can improve the credibility of your product and add another way you can deliver it to potential customers. These sites get unmatched amounts of visitors every day looking to buy products. Why not sell them yours!

9. Listen to your customers! By monitoring your customer feedback and communicating with them you're able to show your customers that you care about their opinions and their thoughts on how to improve future releases. People want to feel like their heard. If you can do that you'll gain many repeat customers just on that basis alone.

CONCLUSION

There's a thousand different ways to make money online. If you run across some other methods not mentioned above even better. The more revenue streams you can produce the safer you're online business will be. I believe that when dealing with an online business, diversification is the key to success. The Internet is a rapidly evolving creature and sometimes things that once worked become obsolete and new methods are created. I urge you to follow this guide and grow your business at a comfortable pace. Riches won't come over night but with hard work, intelligent planning, money management and persistence they will come eventually. Good luck and here's to your success!

Made in the USA
Columbia, SC
24 October 2018